MW00815307

Restoring the Male Image

A Look from the Inside Out

Alex O. Ellis

Copyright © 2007 by Alex O. Ellis

RESTORING THE MALE IMAGE
by Alex O. Ellis

Printed in the United States of America

All rights reserved solely by the author. The author guarantees all contents are original and do not infringe upon the legal rights of any other person or work. Contents and/or cover may not be reproduced in whole or in part in any form without the express written consent of the Author. The views expressed in this book are not necessarily those of the publisher.

Unless otherwise indicated, all scripture quotations are taken from the New King James Version of the Bible © 1979, 1980, 1982 by Thomas Nelson, Inc. Used by permission. All rights reserved.
Cover designed by pmillergraphics@aol.com.

HAT'S OFF TO RESTORING THE MALE IMAGE...

"Brilliant! Classy! Excellent! In *Restoring the Male Image,* Alex gallantly addresses the issue of fashion from an insightful perspective—From the Inside-Out. Thank you Alex for brilliantly reflecting the mirror within and clothing us with the tools needed to be men of distinction."

—Bishop George Searight, Abundant Life Family Worship Church, New Brunswick, NJ

"Alex Ellis, clothier extraordinaire, is a dapper young man that carries the mantle of excellence. He has been gifted with the ability to restore, the artistry of sophistication, that was once embodied by the Renaissance Man."

—Bishop Thomas Weeks III, Global Destiny www.bishopweeks.com

"Love it. Love it. LOVE it! This book is what the world needs to advance to a state of excellence. Alex's view on styling has always been amazing, but to now have the principles laid out plainly is a dream come true. This book will alter your thought patterns which will ultimately change your LIFE!"

—Tye Tribbett, Gospel Recording Artist

"Alex Ellis is a man with style, substance and a message for the masses. As I watch him proclaim His message, one begins to see a beautiful portrait of mission and ministry melded in high style. Ellis is on-point, and uses I.M.A.G.E. powered by imagination that can only be inspired by God. To get his points across, Ellis reminds us that true manhood begins in a much deeper place, and must be packaged in such a way that others are drawn by the very thing they want for themselves: poise, purpose and a passion for people."

—Andria Hall, Award-winning veteran journalist,
President of www.speakeasymedia.com,
and Author of *This Far by Faith* and *The Walk at Work*

A Heartfelt Thanks...

To THOSE WHO CONTRIBUTED their time, opinions, and knowledge by providing insightful dialogue on the importance and influence of IMAGE. The list below represents targeted participants ranging three generations.

Arch Bishop Delano Ellis, *Pentecostal Church of Christ, Cleveland, OH*

Tye Tribbett, *Gospel Recording Artist, Camden, NJ*

Lloyd Boston, *TV Personality, Author, Fashion Consultant, NY*

Dr. Darcel Dillard-Suite, *M.S. President & Co-founder, Full Circle Health, Bronx, NY*

Michael Jones, M.D., *Lexington Plastic Surgeons, NY*

Lloyd Williams, *President & CEO, Harlem Chamber of Commerce, Harlem, NY*

Clyde Wilder, *Founder & Director of Harlem Swingers Dance Group, Harlem, NY*

Voza Rivers, *Executive Producer of New Heritage Theater Group, Harlem, NY*

Johnathan Boyd, *Music Producer, Songwriter, Hillside, NJ*

Mark Provost, *President, Slide Clothing, Manasquan, NJ*

Emanuel Scott, *High School Student, Levittown, PA*

DEDICATION

I would like to dedicate this book to my mom and dad. Dad, you have been a shining example of the image of manhood. You always worked hard, cared for your family, and instilled godly values in all of us. Your wisdom is unparalleled and has guided me through some of the most difficult moments in my life. Your strength, tenacity, and care for people are the godly characteristics I admire the most. I pray that I make you half as proud as your son, as I am to call you "Dad."

Mom, your undying care and support are only rivaled by God's love for me. You have been a faithful cheerleader even in the games I lost in life. Thanks for pushing me to my destiny and never allowing me to settle. I didn't always see it, but now it is so clear. I would have never made it this far without you. May you reap one hundredfold of all that you have invested in me.

CONTENTS

FOREWORD...

ABOUT 15 YEARS AGO, during the time I lived in Brooklyn, New York, instead of parking my car on the street, I paid to keep it at St. Marks Park, a secured parking lot around the corner from my home in Prospect Heights. St. Marks Park was a black-owned business, which appealed to me as the editor-in-chief of *Black Enterprise*, almost as much as knowing that I wouldn't have to get up an hour early before work to find a legal parking space the next morning (thanks to alternate-side-of-the-street parking rules in effect four days a week). Most importantly St. Marks Park was extremely well run, with excellent customer service. One of the attendants they employed, a young brother named Steve, was particularly polite and respectful to me, as well as my wife and children. During the more than four years that I was a St. Marks Park customer, Steve never failed to address me as "Mr. Edmond"—except once.

One early Saturday afternoon, accompanied by then *Black Enterprise* Managing Editor Matthew Scott, I approached the security gate of St. Marks Park and rang the bell. The minute Steve saw us at the gate a scowl immediately crossed his face. As he walked up to the gate, he growled, "What do you want?" Taking no notice of his hostile demeanor, I replied, "Hey Steve. I'm here to get my car." Making no move to unlock the gate, Steve's retort was, "Whose car? You don't have a car in here!" I can't believe it—it's like he doesn't even know me! "Steve, it's me—Mr. Edmond, from over on Prospect Place. I drive that candy apple red Dodge Intrepid right over there!" Not bothering to look at the car I was pointing to, Steve took a half a step closer, and the scowl slowly faded into a sheepish grin of recognition. "I'm sorry, Mr. Edmond—I didn't realize that was you. Step right in."

What happened? For more than three years, Steve had only seen me wearing the standard daily apparel required of all male employees of Earl G. Graves Ltd, the publisher of *Black Enterprise*. As a senior manager of the company, my workday attire consists of a business suit, a dress shirt (often with French cuffs), a necktie (straight or bow), highly polished leather dress shoes and accessories such as cuff links and a pocket square. This, to Steve, is Mr. Edmond. On that one exceptional occasion, Matthew Scott (a family friend and colleague since our undergraduate years at Rutgers University) and I were on our way to another neighborhood for an afternoon of pick-up basketball. We were dressed accordingly: baggy shorts, tank tops, basketball shoes, head and wristbands (Matt) and a red bandana as headgear (me). To Steve, we were two unknown young black males (Matt, in his early 30s at the time, looked exactly as he did as a college freshman), probably gang affiliated, judging from my bandana—trying to go where we were not welcome and had no business. The fact that we were both college graduates, nationally recognized business journalists and two of the top editors on the staff of an award-winning national business publication—not to mention the fact that Steve had known me for more than two years at that point—meant absolutely nothing. His job was to keep "typical brothers" like us OUT!

This story is just one of many personal experiences that have reinforced my understanding of the message Alex O. Ellis so earnestly delivers in the book you now hold in your hands, *Restoring the Male Image: A Look From the Inside Out*. It matters how we as men, particularly black men, present ourselves to the world. In fact, if Steve the parking lot attendant had been Steve the police officer that summer, it could have been the difference between life and death. But the thing is, I've always known my image mattered. I learned that from the way my mother Virginia Edmond, a divorced, single woman raising four children while on public assistance, insisted that my brother and I dress in a suit jacket, dress shirt and tie for our class pictures, when our elementary school classmates were allowed to wear jeans and casual shirts. I learned when she insisted on the same dress code for Sunday church services, stepping into the void left by our absent father to teach my brother and I how to tie a real necktie. We ditched our clip-ons long before we finished elementary school.

Since then I've found that it matters that I own a tuxedo, with patent leather shoes and a few formal cuff-link and studs sets. It matters that I know how to tie a bow tie. I ditched my clip-on bows and spent all day teaching myself to tie a real one on Labor Day 1986, after I was informed by my employer at the time, the publisher of a now-defunct fashion and lifestyle magazine, that clip-on bow ties were for proms and tacky weddings—not for editors of men's fashion magazines. It matters that, as a senior manager and officer of a company founded by one of the most successful and iconic entrepreneurs in America, *Black Enterprise* Founder and Publisher Earl G. Graves, I understand that if I want to do business, I have to come dressed for the occasion, just as a soldier is dressed and equipped with the proper accessories for battle. To quote Mr. G, "At Black Enterprise, I'll accept nothing less than the most professional business attire from every employee, from our operations and administrative staff to our senior management team. There are no dress-down days at our offices, and as far as I'm concerned, there never will be. This is not just about my personal preferences; it's about what's best for business."

None of this is about fashion for the sake of outward appearance alone. A $3,000 business suit, $200 shirt, $125 tie and $250 shoes worn by a slothful, dishonest and unreliable man is false advertisement—a mediocre gift-wrapped in excellence. But it is just as much a misrepresentation to claim to be an honest, talented, responsible person with a strong work ethic, and then clothe yourself shoddily and carelessly in a way that does not reflect the commitment to excellence that is within you. My mother and others who mentored and developed me understood that remaking my outward presentation was about reflecting and reinforcing my growing inner confidence, talent, strength and knowledge of my own value and ability. It meant taking the Godly potential that I was born with and teaching me to let it shine. It was a truly holistic makeover that transformed a poor black boy born under disadvantaged circumstances (by worldly standards) into a productive contributor to society, a successful professional, a committed husband, an involved and dedicated father and most importantly, a man rooted in the legacy of God's excellence.

Restoring The Male Image makes a compelling and passionate case for the idea that personal presentation is not just about the image and style, but the spirit and substance of a man. His book provides the necessary framework for laying the foundation—or achieving the restoration—of potent, productive and positive manhood, as a matter of not just clothing the flesh, but adorning the spirit. As we lament the peril of our young men, labeling them "an endangered species," it is critical that we help them make the connection between their spiritual identity and their outward representation of themselves, and by extension, their Creator, in whose image they were made. This is the gift that my mother, Mr. Graves and others gave me by insisting on an outer presentation that accurately represented the inner substance of personal excellence. It is the gift that I am working hard to share with my only son (who, at age 15, knows what it means to wear French cuffs, cuff links and a pocket square), and my three daughters, who need a way to discern the difference between mediocrity and excellence in the men they will encounter as they enter womanhood.

With *Restoring the Male Image*, Alex Ellis makes an invaluable contribution to my efforts, and that of other parents, role models, educators and mentors seeking tools to encourage productivity, accountability and excellence in our young men. This book must be included in the library of every man who is serious about presenting his best self to the world, as a creature made in God's image and for His purpose.

—Alfred A. Edmond Jr., Sr. VP/Editor-in-Chief
BLACK ENTERPRISE *Magazine*

Introduction

WHAT MAKES A MAN emulate the style of another man? Why is it that the man dressed in a tailored suit and tie is upgraded to first class, over the man in jeans and a T-shirt? What makes a man enter a room and command attention without uttering a word, while his colleague goes unnoticed? The answer to these questions and more lie in the power of his image.

A man's image is one of his most alluring characteristics. People constantly assess you based on your image, and at first glance make decisions about you based on your clothing, grooming and hairstyle. Your image speaks on your behalf before any character trait or personality comes forth. Whether you are a man of integrity, a diligent worker, or a compassionate humanitarian, your style of dress sends a signal to others whether you mean business or if you are wasting their time. The man who wears his "power suit" is serious about his image, even if it is for the day, because his goal is to take care of business. Even though his suit is only an article of clothing, it gives him the confidence to handle the challenges in his dealings with others and determines how they will receive him. The more effort you put into improving your image, the more control you have over the opportunities that come your way both personally and professionally.

My desire is to revive a pride in personal image both internally and externally. I am reminiscent of a time when men and women truly cared about their appearance and took pride in how they looked before they left home. One of my most influential eras for fashion is *The Harlem Renaissance Era (1920s – mid 1930s)*. This was a time when people of all races and cultures, whether rich or poor, dressed like each day was the most important, purposeful day of their life. Men wore dress shirts, ties, jackets and hats while ladies wore dresses, hats and gloves. Despite the racism and other social inequities, *The Harlem Renaissance Era* was a time when Blacks and West Indians particularly looked their best and strutted their stuff. There was such meticulousness about getting dressed back then. You could see your reflection on another man's shined shoes. I want to challenge you to see that the Renaissance man is a mindset—a way of thinking. It is a lifestyle. It is packaged with an internal pride. Renaissance men were proud of who they were individually, culturally, and spiritually. That internal pride exuded out of their being and subsequently was reflected in their external image.

I began this project on image with you in mind because I believe it is an important subject for the young and old alike. It is a subject that is serious, yet not taken seriously. As you will see, my view on image is not just the external appearance we tend to focus on, but I want to tap into a holistic, internal image as well. Far too many of us are preoccupied with our outer appearance and never spend time discovering who we are internally—which is truly what makes us unique.

I created an acronym for the word Image: **I**=Integrity; **M**=Manhood; **A**=Authority; **G**=Generosity; **E**= Excellence. My desire is that these words trigger questions in your mind and force you to revisit your image and ask yourself if your image is in line with who you really are. Consider whether you are exhibiting characteristics for others to emulate as you move towards your destiny. Destiny is time sensitive, so it is important to move towards it now! There are things you aspire to accomplish in life that must be accomplished within a certain time frame. Some opportunities are only here for a season, so it's imperative that you reassess your appearance as soon as possible. When you dress for success your encounters tend to be more favorable; whether it's interviewing for your dream job, networking with key people who can open doors, or making a speech to an influential audience.

Thinking about your image should put you in a serious mindset. Carefully consider the occasion because you naturally perform with a higher level of confidence when you are prepared and are sharply dressed. Not only does your image affect your perception of yourself, but it also impacts other people's perception of you as well. It lends credibility to the essence of who you are. Whether you are selling clothing, real estate, insurance or in banking, your image is a direct correlation to your personal success. When you walk into a department store and the sales representative is dressed well, it increases your trust in that person to help you choose the right style and make informed buying decisions based on your line of work or need for the items. Dressing unprofessionally may distract others from seeing your value and skills, and project a negative image for both you and the company you represent. On the other hand, dressing professionally may cause people to subconsciously associate your personal grooming and clothing with knowledge, reliability, and a strong work ethic. Unfortunately, your true character may be the total opposite. If you identify with this then I would encourage you to read further and seriously consider the internal questions discussed in this book to see how you can improve your internal image in order to be the complete package, both inside and out. If you genuinely want to change you will be successful. Remember, your goal is to make a lasting first impression that is genuine and sincere. If people engage you based on a false first impression, you are on your way to tarnishing your reputation, which will lead to other problems down the road.

Maintaining your image requires constant effort. Be consistent so that others will begin to analyze you based on past positive experiences. Once you establish the appropriate image, be sure to protect it because it is invaluable. I envision my Mastercard® commercial would say: Getting the job $145,000. Treating all your buddies to dinner to celebrate $472.00. Shopping at Brooks Brothers for your first day's new suit $1,289.00. The value of your image "Priceless."

After reading this book you will be well on your way to revisiting your image, and searching within yourself to determine what you need to change in order to enhance the way people perceive you and how you perceive yourself. So step right up and let's get started…

PART I

A VIEW FROM WITHIN

Chapter 1

What Lies Beneath

"What is real is not the external form, but the essence of things...
it is impossible for anyone to express anything essentially
real by imitating its exterior surface."
- Constantin Brancusi, Sculptor

A S MEN WE ARE often judged by our exterior. Whether it's the car we drive, the clothes we wear, how much money we make, or whether our bodies are well defined. What people see creates a strong mental impression of who they think we are. Unfortunately, in our society material possessions have become the measuring tool for men. People fail to realize that there is so much more to us than what's on the outside. I have known men, myself included, who have acquired the acceptable status based on what he owns, yet is still self-conscious, immature, or just plain unhappy with himself. I'm reminded of a childhood story which taught me a valuable lesson that still holds true today.

Although my parents are country folks from the South, I grew up a city boy in New Jersey. Every summer we spent a few weeks at my grandparent's house in North Carolina. I looked forward to the southern traditions because there were always family barbeques and I got a chance to snap peas and shuck corn in the backyard. The highlight for me was picking watermelon. This was not your normal supermarket excursion. My dad would actually drive me and a few of my cousins to Dean's Farm about 10 miles away. Once we got there, my cousins and I would ride on this old rickety school bus that would take us to the far end of the farm where the watermelon patches were. As we traveled down those red clay dirt roads, the bus would shake and the coils in the seats would bounce us clear up to the ceiling! There was something special about being on a farm as a kid.

Once the bus driver parked and let us off, my cousins and I scoured the red clay aisles in search of the perfect watermelon. No other fruit says summertime like watermelon. As far as my eyes could see, there were watermelons everywhere! As I turned to go down another aisle I saw it from a distance. The biggest watermelon I had ever seen. I screamed, "Daddy, Daddy I FOUND IT! I found the watermelon!" He ran towards me and said, "Wow son, you sure picked a big one!" My dad proceeded to shake the watermelon and then he thumped it with his finger. He explained to us that if it is ripe it will have a certain sound. This gigantic watermelon looked and sounded good, so dad cut it from the vine and threw it on the bus.

Once we got back to my grandparent's house we hosed off the watermelon and put it in the icebox. After dinner it was time for some good ol' country watermelon. My dad covered the picnic table in the backyard with newspaper and placed the watermelon on it. He pulled out a knife, as if he was a Ninja Warrior, and began to split the watermelon down the middle. By now, my cousins and I were salivating because we couldn't wait to dive into the first slice of cold, juicy watermelon. As the two halves fell apart we all gasped because the watermelon was dark red and mushy inside! Everyone was disappointed. My eyes began to fill with so much water that the next blink would send streams gushing down my face. "But Daddy you said that it was a good watermelon," I whined. He replied, "I know son, I thought it was. It looked good, felt good, and even sounded good, but there was something messed up inside." That day, at the tender age of six I learned a lesson that would stick with me some 30 years later. I learned that you can't judge anything based on its outward appearance alone. The watermelon had all of the characteristics of being ripe fruit, but its exterior was deceptive—like many people.

On the outside it is easy for a man to present the perfect package, whether he is dressing for an interview or going on a date. He can dress to the epitome of distinction for an interview, but have no interest in the company vision. The company executives are under the impression that he is coming on board for the long haul when in actuality his true motivation is to use this company as a stepping stone to get where he really wants to go. On the other hand, when a man dresses for a date, he can look like everything a woman ever wanted. He can be a sharp dresser, drum up intriguing conversation, and sweep her off her feet in a matter of minutes, but underneath it all he may be driven by an ulterior motive. Despite my early lesson in life, I eventually wound up living out my own watermelon story.

Looking back at my teenage years, I recall being in the gifted and talented program in high school. I got good grades and participated in several clubs: The Math Club, Science Club, Minorities In Engineering and Student Council to name a few. I was an intelligent kid who was hard working and charismatic. My above average height led people to believe that I was a star basketball player. That assumption was far from the truth. I was very skinny, non-athletic and had no muscular definition. I became very self-conscious and developed an inferiority complex. To top it off, my parents couldn't afford the trendy clothes that I desired. I wore goofy steel framed, black trimmed glasses. I hated how I looked yet I couldn't hide because my height brought unavoidable attention. I was ridiculed and called names like "nerd" and "punk." Although I was an outsider with the "popular" teenagers, I did have a close circle of friends who, much like me, had good grades, but were also outsiders with their own area of *perceived* deficiency.

I subconsciously stooped over in hopes of blending in, while others wished they could be as tall as me. It just goes to show that we are never truly happy with the qualities God gives us. I went to gym class one day and my teacher said, "Why are you slouching? Stand up straight! Push your shoulders back; be proud to be tall!" Until this conversation I never realized what I was doing. She was so right. I was not mature enough to be comfortable in my own skin.

After graduating from high school, I was accepted into North Carolina A&T State University. It was important for me to get away from the negativity in high school, other people's opinions of me, and my own self imposed limitations. Sometimes change is good. I needed a fresh start. North Carolina was a nine hour drive from New Jersey, so it was far enough that no one else knew me. This would be a new beginning for Alex. By this time I was 6'3" and I figured I might as well be the sharpest, tallest brother they ever saw, and I was. For years I strove to look my absolute best. I hid behind designer labels, fine clothes, and expensive accessories, yet buried underneath my perfected external image, I was still very broken inside.

After returning home from college I remember a life changing evening when a close friend confronted me with questions about how I felt about myself and my infatuation with clothing. Her interrogation forced me to look in the mirror and ask myself some really soul searching questions. She said, "What are you trying to cover up? What is it about yourself that you don't like?" I reluctantly admitted all the things I didn't like about myself, like I was too thin, and not muscular or athletic like the other guys. I broke down sobbing because no matter how I dressed, underneath the clothes I didn't like what I saw. I came to realize that I struggled with low self-esteem for a large part of my life. She reinforced my great inner qualities and reminded me that I was made in the image and likeness of God. She told me that I was intelligent, creative, and a man of great purpose. After she counseled me for about an hour we prayed and I asked God to help me to see myself as He sees me. That night He began the process of restoring my self-esteem. I must admit, it didn't happen overnight, but thank God I was on the road to recovery!

God answered my prayers. I began to see myself as he saw me, and that had nothing to do with what I wore and everything to do with who He created me to be. So there was a shift and the internal became the priority. As I began to walk in this new perspective there were several steps I had to take:

1. I had to **first** admit I had an issue.
2. I had to take the time to discover who I was.
3. I had to identify someone who would be honest with me and would keep me accountable through this process.
4. I had to learn to love myself and accept all of me.
5. I would focus on healing and growing internally more so than dressing the outside.
6. I would not be afraid to seek outside help from a psychologist, life coach, counselor, or member of the clergy.
7. Share my testimony with someone else in hopes that they would also be liberated.

All of these steps took time, yet going through each one, brought about a change in how I perceived myself. I believe if you are in a mode of self doubt that you should try these steps towards your healing.

After coming through that process, my life was indeed different. Nothing externally changed, but I changed my outlook on myself and my life. I was transformed. I didn't get rid of the clothes I loved so much, but now I wore the clothes as opposed to them wearing me. In the past I only felt confident in a three piece suit, yet lacked confidence in jeans and a T-shirt. Now I have the same swagger in khaki's as I do in a custom suit, because the source of my confidence comes from within.

TIE IT ALL IN...

1. Does your image accurately reflect who you are?
2. Have you gained a level of success in the eyes of other people, but have a deep sense of failure or emptiness inside?
3. Do you spend time evaluating your motives?
4. Do you feel pressured to live up to the expectations of others?
5. Do you have a problem developing and maintaining intimate relationships?

The Ellis Bunch: Top from left to right:
Lester Jr. & Sheila, Vincent & Sandra, Alex & Cousin Makilia.

My Steve Urkel moment.

They call me Stretch!

Destined for the Big City. College days.

Chapter 2

FEARFULLY AND
WONDERFULLY MADE

*"As we are raising our children we have to affirm them.
If a boy has kinky hair you have to affirm the kinky hair.
If he has no hair you have to affirm the baldness. You have to
really remind him that God made him in His image and you
know we all look so different, well imagine what
God looks like!"*
-Dr. Darcel Dillard-Suite

L ACK OF SELF ESTEEM is one of the biggest challenges
facing our youth today, especially our black males. Dr. Suite
stresses the importance of getting rid of the perception that young
men must wear designer clothing to validate themselves, as name
brands have a strong influence on young people's idea of image.

We must begin to build a solid foundation in our youth by
revealing who they were created to be and the limitless potential
they possess. We must encourage our youth to participate in
extra curricular activities, arts, missions trips, culture, and the
theatre. All of these things build an esteem that is not based on
performance, material things, or even their physiques. I too have
been guilty of debating with young people about their diverse
styles. I've commented to young men that their clothing is too

baggy or to young ladies that their clothing is too revealing. I believe that we must celebrate the uniqueness and creativity of our youth. At the same time we must let them know that there has to be some standards and boundaries in their lives that should not be compromised.

To only address the external is to deal with the manifestation of a much deeper issue inside of them. We must instill enough confidence inside of them that when their standards are being compromised that they have the fortitude to stand on their own. They must be careful not to assimilate because it is what everyone else is doing. If not their true identity will succumb to society's pressure to replicate its image, as opposed to being their own unique self. Today's youth have to find their true identity through parents, role models, teachers and self discovery.

I spoke with Dr. Suite on the problems affecting our youth, particularly young men, and what her clinic is doing to combat these issues.

A.E.: What part do you think we play as adults in helping to bring an end to low self-esteem in young people?

Dr. Suite: Self-esteem is deeper than what you look like and what you're wearing. Self-esteem is also how you feel about you. So you've got to affirm and also impart positive energy into the person growing up. Let them make choices and don't tear them down when they make the choice that you may not agree with. You can actually use the power of their words to have a positive impact on their self-esteem.

A.E.: What topics or activities do you cover in your life skills groups?

Dr. Suite: In life skills we deal with perception, self-esteem, finances, anger, and self control. We focus on the 9 principles that are part of the Fruit of the Spirit [*Galatians*]. We try to use these principles in our life skills class to educate people about how there is so much power in the essence of who they are.

A.E.: In our earlier discussions you mentioned that image and self-esteem are important—especially to the young black men. Are the counseling sessions on image gender based?

Dr. Suite: No. Any counseling we do while customized can be done by a male or female when dealing with self-esteem. What we find important and constant is "respect." We make sure the young male is respected and appreciated for who he is. We do make an effort to make sure that even when young men are matched with our female counselors that they are seen and also follow-up with our male senior clinical team—so that they do see a black male in the practice. We have a team approach and this works well.

A.E.: What are some of the challenges men are facing today?

Dr. Suite: Unemployment plagues our society but none are hit harder than our young black men—especially those with limited skills and education. During our counseling, if we determine that this is an issue, we connect them with community partners who will help place them. They also work with them on this aspect of their healing process—not having a job can very easily become a mental health issue! What we have learned is that by just connecting them with others who care and are invested in their success helps rebuild an already broken motivation around employment possibilities.

A.E.: Describe the typical background of the males in your sessions?

Dr. Suite: The breakdown is: 1) adolescent males 14-18 years old, single parent home (typically there is a mother, no father and a few siblings or stepbrothers and sisters, high school education, struggling to stay in school, and anger issues); 2) adult population 25 and up, successful employment, college education, unmarried and dealing with depression; 3) men 35 and up, dealing with broken relationships—and in need of a good support system!

Overall, my discussions with Dr. Suite confirmed that both young and older black men are in crisis. The crisis has various other components which include unemployment, lack of education and inadequate healthcare. It is important to educate ourselves on the problems affecting our men today and partner with community programs, churches and organizations like Dr. Suite's to help alleviate this dilemma.

 TIE IT ALL IN...

1. Are you able to appreciate your own accomplishments and good deeds?
2 Do you have difficulty expressing your feelings?
3. Do you isolate yourself from other people?
4. Are you initially shy and withdrawn in new social settings?
5. Do you hold on to friendships (even bad ones) because you fear being alone or abandoned?

Chapter 3

IMITATIONS OF LIFE

*"The greatest difficulty is that men do not think
enough of themselves, do not consider what it is that
they are sacrificing when they follow in a herd,
or when they cater for their establishment."*
- Ralph Waldo Emerson, Poet, Essayist

THE DESIRE TO FIT in the crowd is a real struggle for both youth and adults. Our youth are affected by the same never-ending quest to be in the "in crowd." Nearly everyone is trying to keep up with the Jones' and they are starting younger and younger. Adults desire the mini-mansion and luxury cars while our youth demand the latest sneakers, jeans, and jewelry. Both are willing to do anything to keep up the status quo—even if it's illegal. Young people are going into extreme debt to support their copycat habits. They risk their future to fund a flashy lifestyle. Externally, they have the image they desired, but how much did it really cost? Often times it costs much more than the value of money because you cannot put a price tag on dignity and integrity. In the long run, if you continue chasing after the "in crowd" you will end up surrounded by people who love you for what you have as opposed to genuinely loving you for who you are.

Having the latest designer pieces and enough ice to keep you cold in June would be fulfilling enough for anyone, right? Wrong!

That's not real life. Spending all that you own in an attempt to imitate someone else will still leave you unfulfilled, because you are not being true to who you really are. And to top it all off, then you read in the papers the person you are having plastic surgery to look like, is checking into rehab because he isn't happy with who he is himself! Not to mention the fact that many of the images we see are digitally enhanced–that is they are far from the real thing. All that glitters isn't gold! Real life isn't in the abundance of things. You can lead a life full of all of the trappings of success, but if you never fulfill your purpose, your life is in vain. Fulfilling your purpose is the key ingredient to attaining wholeness.

A recent study looked at the depression in adolescence specifically children between the ages of twelve and seventeen. More than 7% of boys and almost 14% of girls had met the full circle criteria for depression. One factor leading to this rate of depression could be the young person's desire to attain the status and image of their celebrity role models.

Culturally, we are obsessed with our outward appearance. Every day we are bombarded with movies, commercials, and advertisements that entice us to fit an image that is deemed appropriate by society. Women and men go to great lengths and undergo various plastic surgeries in an attempt to find the perfect image, while the internal well-being has fallen by the wayside. We attract people based on our outward appearance, yet because we lack wholeness within, we often settle for unhealthy relationships.

In an era of reality TV and *Extreme Makeover*, plastic surgeons and ordinary citizens have become celebrities. What used to be a hobby for the rich and famous has shifted to the average person diligently saving their money for a physical transformation. Plastic surgery was once thought of as a woman's procedure. More alarming is the fact that since the year 2000 male plastic surgery increased by 30%. This includes hair transplants, laser peels and other skin resurfacing procedures. The popular wrinkle reducer Botox has seen a 162% increase in use for both men and women since 2001. Parents are opting in for more of their teenagers to become surgically enhanced as well. With regard to trends based on ethnicity, Caucasians still lead the way with nearly 80% of all procedures, while Asian are at 9%, Blacks at 7%, and Hispanics at 18%. The total increase in percentages by ethnic group from 2004-2005 are Caucasians 4.9% blepharoplasty: upper or lower eyelids and rhinoplasty: nose jobs, Asians 26.7% blepharoplasty, Blacks 48.6% rhinoplasty and Hispanic 88.9% rhinoplasty and blepharoplasty.

I was fortunate to speak with Dr. Michael Jones, a board certified plastic surgeon to hear his perspective on the upsurge in male plastic surgery throughout the country.

A.E.: Is plastic surgery a growing trend for men of color?

Dr. Jones: In the last five years I have seen a significant increase in the number of Black men coming forward for cosmetic procedures. They come in for Botox, collagen, face peels, rhinoplasty, and liposuction. Probably the next biggest thing would be eye surgery because we as men tend to show a lot of our aging around our eyes. Whether its bags under the eyes, drooping eyelids, or puffy eyes, we have procedures to remedy all of that.

A.E.: Do you think the increased procedures are driven by our compulsion to replicate the images that we see in Hollywood?

Dr. Jones: No. I don't think men are trying to emulate what they see. Men in this generation are still concerned about their image, and they want to workout, look good, and be appealing to their mate. What has happened now is that plastic surgery has become more prominent and men have access to more information, so they are less scared about coming forward. It is not unlike going to your tailor or like getting your nails done even as men. Now they are less apprehensive about asking for it. There is definitely a difference between the reasons why men and women get plastic surgery. Most women are looking for that star quality, whereas men are more concerned with maintaining their looks.

In essence, there is an identity crisis that exists within many of us. We often imitate others because we genuinely feel they are better than we are and totally underestimate the values within ourselves. As adults, we have to make a concerted effort to encourage the generation behind us and declare their positive values and abilities so they will not wander aimlessly on a quest to imitate a false reality portrayed by society.

 TIE IT ALL IN...

1. Do you feel the need for approval from others?
2. Are you afraid of criticism?
3. Do you find yourself wearing particular clothing because of others as opposed to your own style?
4. Are you a follower or do you blaze your own trail?

PART II

IN FULL VIEW

Chapter 4

THE "EYES" HAVE IT

*"Your image transmits a message about you all day every day.
There is no erase button."*
—Susan Bixler

A S LONG AS GOD continues to bless you with eyesight,
you are constantly assessing someone. Every time you blink,
your brain instantly sends mental pictures about the person in front
of you, especially their style of dress. By nature, human beings are
visual creatures, and people formulate their opinion of you in a
matter of seconds based on how you look.

When you feel good about your appearance, it shows. If you
believe you have the right look for the occasion then you are likely
to act with a higher level of confidence and by all means put your
best foot forward. In Robert Greene's bestselling work, *The 48
Laws of Power* he states, "Everything is judged by appearance; what
is unseen counts for nothing." Mr. Greene has carved his niche
as an authority on getting ahead in corporate America. I don't
necessarily condone many of his laws and tactics, however, his no
nonsense formula works well in the corporate arena. I particularly
agree with *Law #5 "So Much Depends on Reputation- Guard It With
Your Life"* and *Law #6 "Court Attention At All Costs"* as they both key
in on realistic, yet not overly cynical approaches to creating and
protecting your image. As we delve further into appearance we will

touch on the importance of establishing and maintaining a good reputation. A good name goes a long way. Protect your name as if your life depends on it because it is really all you have. In addition, Greene's charge to "Court Attention" has its limits. Be careful not to be rude or obnoxious to garner attention. With the right image, you can court attention in a positive, subtle manner.

Everything about you becomes your brand. Once you see yourself as your own personal brand, you can begin to advertise and market your visual image. Just like advertisers are intent on marketing and selling a product, you must make your image your own personal brand. Stay away from co-branding with friends and family as you can only be accountable for yourself. It is important to take pride in your branded image and sell it everywhere you go. It's what people see and it's what they remember. Even after giving the most profound speech, a disheveled appearance can be distracting.

It is extremely important for men to take charge of their image. We should always look our best even if we are wearing a warm up suit. The dilemma becomes people's perception of you in the warm up suit. Perception becomes the onlooker's reality, and it immediately begins to take shape in their minds. A recent psychological study on the impact of image found that upon meeting someone for the first time it takes 15 seconds for a person to form a laundry list of impressions about your character and abilities. In addition, Marilee Zdenek, Founder and President of Right Brain Resources, Inc. stated, "The moment you alter your perception of yourself and your future, both you and your future begin to change." Her statement confirms the power of perception and the power of your mind. You can truly accomplish anything you put your mind to and obtain successful results, image included.

It is important for me to differentiate between the external and internal image. One of our innate characteristics is our ability to view someone or something externally and form several opinions. Often times, television portrays images of men as slobs or couch potatoes with absolutely no sense of style. I wanted to be clear about what the outer appearance meant to several of the men I interviewed. I discovered that the men believed that their external image was key to the male image persona.

A.E.: What does a man's external image say about him?

Voza Rivers: I think image is an extension of who we are. If we take pride in the way we look it extends our signature in terms of who we are. We must understand that a lot of who people think we are is that visual image that they see before they get to know us. I came up at a time when my grandfather at 19 years of age came from Jamaica. He started working and used to have his clothes made. I followed in his footsteps because he left such an indelible impression on me. There are a group of men that I have grown up with who all remember how important it was to uphold the image that really defined who we were and who we hoped to be. A lot of that was formed by our grandparents and parents and given to us without beating us off over the head. I think image is extremely important. It's not the only thing, but I'm also seeing a shift again where you see some of our leading icons in the music industry, especially with the hip hop generation now putting on ties and suits and clearly are looking back at a page in our history where clothes accompanied the persona of who you are.

Lloyd Boston: For me image is a total consciousness of my being. Of course clothing and accessories would be the kind of obvious translation most people see each day. I've always believed that clothing isn't really a second skin. Many people think it is second skin yet I think of it as a primary skin, unless you're living in a nudist colony! Most people aren't running around naked so your clothing really is your primary skin. However, many people don't prioritize their image. Sometimes it's an afterthought. I think when you prioritize it, you put more energy into choosing what to wear or feature—especially accessories.

Tye Tribbett: Image means perception. You can draw a conclusion of someone's personality based on their image. If you have on a wave cap and a hoodie—someone might draw a conclusion that you are from the hood. Image is the first impression people have of you.

Clyde Wilder: I guess because of my upbringing and from where I came from (*Harlem*) I like to be clean and sharp. I like to present myself in a strong manner. I like when people see me and they say, "Wow! Nice!" to what I have on and how I present myself. It stems from what my family gave me, and its what I want to present each time that I appear in public. Whether it's a performance or just hanging out, I like to be sharp, no matter what attire I have on or the occasion. If it's African attire or if it's regular European clothing or whatever, I just got to look good. It's a complete package.

Arch Bishop Delano Ellis: Preachers in the modern age have become so conscious of their fashion image that they forgot that there was a prescribed look and behavior. Now if we go back through scripture we discover that we were forbidden to dress like everybody else. We were called upon to be uniquely different and to be uniquely set apart. What I decided to do is design my life and conduct around what is called traditional priesthood so I skew pretty much to the line of tradition. Of course every now and then Alex and my wife can step in and pull me out!

Mark Provost: I think image really says something about the way a person is. It really embodies the being of a person. It's what that person may be trying to impress upon everybody around him. If they're getting dressed for the night in designer suits, funky shoes, and a real cool shirt they may be trying to express their personality through their clothes. I buy and design things that I am trying to project in my company. I want people to really think about what they're wearing and let their clothes express their feelings.

Overall, I found that regardless of age, gender and occupation, these men see image as a vital part of their being. It is an expressive mode of dress and personal attributes that form others' opinion of you.

 TIE IT ALL IN...

1. How much time do you spend on your personal appearance? Do you think you need to spend more or less time? Why?

2. What message do you intend for your clothes to convey about you?

3. Do people compliment you on your clothing? How often?

4. Do you have a power suit? If yes, consider adding new accessories. If no, its time to invest in one.

ABRACADABRA

"Reputation has a power like magic:
with one stroke of its wand, it can double your strength.
It can also send people scurrying away from you."
-Robert Greene

ABSOLUTELY EVERYONE SHOULD ASPIRE to attain a good reputation. As the saying goes, "Your reputation precedes you" so always strive for perfection. The more you hone and work on your reputation, the less work you will have to do once it is established. Your reputation speaks to the quality of life you live or the work ethic you possess. As people come in contact with you they form opinions and the consensus of those opinions leads to your reputation, whether good or bad. The challenge with reputation is that it is often formulated by what you allow people to see. If you act unseemly in public just one time, people will always expect that of you and instantly begin to lose respect for you. Not to mention the rumor mill that begins to spread if one person sees you and then tells someone else. By the time it trickles back to you, your actions may be misrepresented beyond repair. Imagine if hundreds or thousands see you? Trust me you have an uphill battle trying to prove otherwise. Just think about it, if you are known for being a man of integrity or a hard worker, and then one day a story comes out in the local paper citing tax evasion and claiming that your climb up the corporate ladder was based on nepotism. Your reputation will quickly spiral downward and people will never look at you the same way—even if it is false. Instead, people will gossip and exaggerate more stories of misdeeds regardless of its truth.

Remember, prior to the rumor mill, you had a strong reputation. When it came time for companies to decide who to do business with, you didn't have to send additional fruit baskets or box seat tickets to win the business. Now you have to devote a great deal of time, money and energy to reclaim your good name. Men in the spotlight are frequently placed in Catch 22 situations protecting their reputation. On the one hand, they may make a decision to take the high road and not respond to false allegations. Conversely, if they choose to deny the allegations they often appear guilty and other issues of their character and reputation begin to surface and opens up other cans of worms.

Likewise, the reputation of a corporation can truly make or break its success. One false PR mishap like animal testing or misleading labels can send the company's stock plummeting. The public gravitates and associates with corporations as if they are people. The old adage, "The Customer is Always Right" still holds true today as corporations continue to expend resources on Customer Relationship Management (CRM) Software solutions. CRM is the new software buzzword which allows companies to track customer activity and retain every characteristic about the customer including spending habits, complaints, as well as birthdays, anniversaries or other key milestones.

Reputation and character go hand in hand. Character holds us to a higher level of accountability in our lives. Character differs from reputation in that it goes deeper than who people perceive you to be, but reveals who you really are inside. "Our character is what we do when we think no one is looking." – *H. Jackson Brown Jr.* In other words, character says, no one will ever know that I stole this money, but my personal convictions hold me to a higher standard; therefore, the money will remain untouched. A person's character will reveal a clearer picture of the true individual. I was watching the news recently and witnessed a very common scenario where a person just committed a heinous crime and the reporters interviewed relatives and neighbors who said they never thought this person was capable of such a crime. It is truly scary to know someone for several years or live with them, and never really know their true character. "Many a man's reputation would not know his character if they met on the street."- Elbert Hubbard.

Habit on the other hand, is something that a person is known to do routinely, without much thought. We all know that we have both good and bad habits. Our good habits like wearing a seatbelt and holding the door for a lady should be commended, while our bad habits such as dropping our clothes around the house or leaving the toilet seat up need to be worked on. Reputation, character and habit are key aspects to consider when taking the step towards improving your image.

TIE IT ALL IN...

1. Do you think your reputation accurately reflects your character? Why or why not?
2. What have you done to create your reputation?
3. What have you done to maintain your reputation?
4. Will most people praise your character or say negative things about you? Why?
5. What bad habits are you willing to work on?

Chapter 5

I.M.A.G.E

"Man looks at the outward, but God looks at the heart."
-1 Samuel 16:7

I DIDN'T WANT TO PAINT a lofty, vague or abstract concept of image so I devised a way to easily recall the fundamental principles of Image: **I=Integrity, M=Manhood, A=Authority, G=Generosity and E=Excellence**.

I = INTEGRITY

"In looking for people to hire, you look for three qualities:
integrity, intelligence, and energy. And if they don't have the first,
the other two will kill you."
- Warren Buffet, Philanthropist

Integrity, like character is who you are when no one else is looking. It's having sound moral principles and exercising them in an upright and honest manner. I believe integrity is an essential part of a person's true image. We are easily impressed by external appearances.

We will spend our last dollar to pretend we are someone else or on another level, but God looks deeper. Yet integrity says I will not try to fool people with a polished exterior. A man desires to be pure in who he is and what he does, so that the external presentation is just a reflection of his internal state. Therefore, integrity can be seen as being true to oneself. I believe integrity is something taught early in life usually by our parents around the same time they instilled moral values in us. It ranks high up there in the Bible's Ten Commandments forbidding us not to steal, lie, or deceive each other. It is a concept that we are faced with every day. Children and young adults are often faced with lying to their parents about grades or dating, while adults are faced with honesty issues like cheating on their income taxes, adultery, and other tempting choices. Regardless of your upbringing, doing the right thing all the time is challenging for everyone.

In 2001, one of the biggest scandals to hit America was the collapse of the energy giant Enron. Confidence in corporate governance was depleted as these corporate executives were more concerned with self enrichment than their employees and shareholders. The men in question appeared to have an impeccable external image. They wore fine suits and carried themselves in a most professional manner. They worked in high level positions and were compensated with six and seven figure incomes. However, they had character flaws that cost them their careers. They were convicted of conspiracy and fraud. Enron's collapse illustrated the loopholes in corporate accounting practices and created legislation which made directors and officers of public corporations more accountable for the company's financial outcome. Companies could no longer inflate earnings like Enron. This case which demonstrated a lack of integrity created a domino affect which not only impacted the executives who were indicted, but also the corporation, its employees, and all those who did business with them.

My goal is not to get you to spend your life rigorously trying to meet a long list of moral do's and don'ts; however, I do want to compel you to take time for self inspection to reevaluate whether or not you are a man of integrity. Not whether you "look" like a man of integrity, but that you truly are a man with personal integrity. Remember it is a matter of the heart. Are you kind to others? Do you take good care of your children? Are you true to the relationships you are involved in? If you answered "no" to any of these questions, make a personal commitment today to take steps to change. Your image will always be flawed unless you make a personal commitment to integrity.

 TIE IT ALL IN...

1. Are you a man of your word?
2. Are you the same person in public as you are in private?
3. Do you speak up in meetings when decisions are made which conflict with your moral values?
4. Are you personally accountable for your actions?

M = MANHOOD

"Masculinity is bestowed. A boy learns who he is and what he's got from a man, or the company of men. He cannot learn it any other place.
He cannot learn it from other boys, and he cannot learn it from the world of women.
The plan from the beginning of time was that his father would lay the foundation for a young boy's heart, and pass on to him that essential knowledge and confidence in his strength. Dad would be the first man in his life, and forever the most important man."

- John Eldredge, Author, "Wild At Heart"

In *Understanding the Power and Purpose of Men*, Dr. Myles Munroe states that God created man to fulfill six distinct purposes. If every man lives out each of these criterion his true purpose as a male would be revealed: (i) visionary, (ii) leader, (iii) teacher, (iv) cultivator, (v) provider and (vi) protector. As I thought about these qualities I reflected on those men who impacted my life and how they fit into each criterion.

(i) Visionary – **Mr. Earl Graves** – As the Founder and CEO of *Black Enterprise Magazine*, he has been a profound example of a visionary in business. Mr. Graves' knowledge and entrepreneurship have motivated me to continue my entrepreneurial endeavors and to personally devote time to empowering people. His undaunting commitment to the empowerment and progression of his people is inspiring. Mr. Graves' vision has had a global impact and he has built a legacy for generations to come.

(ii) Leader- **Bishop George Searight** – My connection to this man of God stems over 13 years. I have been privileged to work closely and serve him both personally and in his ministry. Time and time again he has proven himself to be an exceptional leader and spiritual father. I have watched him lead a congregation of 35 to now well over 4,000 members. As a leader, he has instilled in his congregation to live a life of morality, excellence, empowerment, and most important, to maintain a true commitment to God.

(iii) Teacher – **Pastor Troy Anthony Bronner** – Pastor Bronner's intellectual prowess is second to none. He has been my mentor for several years and has personally taken the time to teach me how to study the *Bible*, interpret scripture, and effectively craft a sermon. I am enriched by Pastor Bronner's impartation of wisdom. I now realize that God places people in your life when you are ready to receive what they have to offer. Pastor Bronner arrived once I was mature enough to value God's instruction.

(iv) Cultivator – **Dr. Warren Dennis** – A cultivator is someone who disturbs your ground and then plants seeds and watches over

them until your ground produces fruit. As my advisor at the New Brunswick Theological Seminary, Dr. Dennis has undoubtedly fulfilled his role above and beyond the call of duty. He has caused me to alter my perspective on my life's purpose and the impact I have on my church, my community and the world. He has broadened my scope and sharpened my view as a world changer. His impartation has shown me my purpose and how I can better serve humanity.

(v) Provider – **Mr. Lester Ellis Sr.** - My father was the epitome of a provider. As the head of our house he made sure we all had what we needed, even if his needs went unmet. We may not have received everything we wanted, but he did an outstanding job, taking care of a wife and five children and I am truly proud of him. He has always been a hard worker and he instilled in me the value of a strong work ethic. My father set the benchmark for what a provider should be, and I am grateful for his wisdom, love and devotion to his family.

(vi) Protector – **Mr. Vincent Lamonte Ellis** – My older brother Vincent was my protector. During my high school years I was not much of a fighter. I didn't have to be because my big brother looked for a reason to beat up somebody who may have called me a name or cut me in the lunch line. Even though I grew much taller than him, I was well protected because they knew I was still "Lil' Vinnie's" brother, and believe me they backed off.

Manhood is a responsibility. It is ownership and accountability for your actions at all times. There comes a time in every male's life where he leaves behind the innocence of childhood. As the Apostle Paul writes, "When I was a child, I spoke as a child, I understood as a child; but when I became a man I put away childish things" (*1 Cor. 13:1*). Throughout history and in many cultures today, boys underwent rites of passage ceremonies to recognize the transition to manhood. But what if there is no ceremony? How are boys supposed to know when they have become a man? Boys began engaging in what society deems "manly" activities such as engaging in sports; having sex; or taking on the macho role around women. Manhood is much more than a masculine physique; it is being a father to your children, a husband to your wife, and a responsible caring person to those around you. It is not about making babies—any boy can do that!

A real man should feel a sense of responsibility to reproduce himself in the life of his own son or other young men. Men must mentor young boys whose fathers were boys themselves that did not stick around to teach basic skills—how to tie a tie, shine your shoes and shave. Finally, manhood is about taking responsibility and being accountable for your actions, and understanding the repercussions for the decisions you make. If that happens at 15-years-old or 30-years-old, then that is your realization into manhood and the only one that you need. There is nothing you can do to make yourself more of a man—either you are or you aren't.

MALE ROLE MODELS

I must admit that my oldest brother Lester Jr. was a role model for me. He was in the Navy and traveled the world for many years. Subsequently, his wardrobe was vast and I was his biggest fan. Once he relocated back to New Jersey, we would travel to New York City on the weekends and visit the finest men's boutiques on Madison Avenue and the surrounding area. He exposed me to a world of fashion that I never knew existed. I could not afford much of anything because I was in high school. He showed me neckties that cost over $100—that was 15 years ago! This had a profound impact on my life and gave me a glimpse into the fashion industry as a career. Once this world was uncovered it created a drive in me to pursue this goal. Many men settle for mediocrity in life because we have not been exposed to anything else. Like me, once I got a taste of what a better life looked like, I knew my current situation was not going to be my permanent residence. I was ready to dream bigger.

Another one of my role models was Pastor Otis Lockett Sr., my pastor while in college at North Carolina A&T. Prior to meeting him, I had never seen a pastor so well dressed. From head to toe he was immaculate. He only wore French cuff shirts, silk Italian ties, and custom made suits. He never overdid his appearance, but always had an eye for detail. Purchasing custom clothing gives you the liberty to stand out in a crowd. Many men who purchase custom clothing tend to go overboard. Being a custom clothier for eight years, I have learned that "less is more." Excellent craftsmanship, quality fabrics, and classic designs go a long way as opposed to extra buttons, outlandish colors, and needless details. I am a huge fan of his timeless style.

In speaking with a few men I asked who their male role models were growing up:

Johnathan Boyd: My male role model that taught me the finer points of haberdashery was Louis D. McCann. He was the sharpest dude ever and still is. He is my favorite uncle. I grew up in his home with his children and he gave my brother and me the tough dad talks. Being late to Sunday School was not an option in my strict Church Of God In Christ household so at about 4 years old he showed me how to tie a tie once and forever. Uncle Lou taught my brother and me how to shine it up, tie it up, tip our brim perfectly, and how to wear cologne. He had me wearing Grey Flannel at 5 years old. Even today, I can't go to the grocery store without throwing on some Chrome or Curve. I also enjoy getting a manicure once a month.

Lloyd Williams: You know the old saying "it takes a village?" It is an old African proverb. Who were those persons for me? It certainly was my father and my teachers. I don't know why I had the opportunity to meet and interface with great role models like Martin Luther King, Jr. and Nelson Mandela. Other great men I interfaced with include Al Sharpton, Jesse Jackson, Max Roach, Miles Davis, Kareem Abdul Jabar, and Earl "The Pearl" Monroe. I'm also honored to have had a tutor, Mr. Hughes, I later discovered that it was none other than Langston Hughes who helped tutor me in English. The most important thing is that it was a village of people that helped me when I needed help, smack me if I needed to be smacked, and direct me if I needed to be directed. My real concern about what I see happening with young people today is they're not involved. They're not members, they don't go to block association meetings, they don't go to school board meetings, they don't go to community board meetings, they're not in the NAACP or they're not with the Urban League. Therefore, their knowledge of the world when they are informed is through 30 second sound bytes as opposed to internal direct information and interfacing with those involved in the issues.

Tye Tribbett: Thank God my father was in my life. My mom taught me how to tie a tie first. I was the kid who wore suits to school everyday. My dad was very influential on my image. His influence helped me win best dressed in school.

Voza Rivers: It started with my father's grandfather. There were several teachers in both parochial and public school. H. Rutgers of the famous Rutgers Basketball Tournament put his hands on so many of us as young men. I learned to play basketball under his tutelage. He was a teacher and a role model for a lot of us. Another role model was Royce Phillips, also a teacher. Another teacher was Ed Carpenter who not only taught me but he also taught my dad at the same school. So there were these male mentors and then later on in life Percy Sutton also put his hand on me and gave me an opportunity to work very closely with him running his record label and management company. There was also Roger Thurman who came out of the American Negro Theater with Ossie Davis, Ruby Dee and Sidney Poitier. He used to tell me stories of how as teenagers they would gather at the basement of a library on 135th Street. Eventually they stepped into prominence, but they were just answering the call to a creative fervor to practice a craft and to learn as much as they could. I never thought acting was my calling card but twenty four years later I'm following in the footsteps of individuals like Ossie Davis and Count Basie. My firm was the business manager for Count Basie. He was the first major client we had. It was so amazing just to sit and listen to him speak with such elegance, grace, commitment, and talent. I was fortunate to be able to listen to stories about a relationship he had with a young Quincy Jones at 19 years of age. I mean these are role models and stories that are indelible in my mind. I believe also that I've inherited this kind of spirituality that connects me to this community based on the fact that I'm on *Strivers Row*. I'm in the entertainment business. I'm in the cultural business. The very first African American owned record label was at 255 W. 138th Street, I'm at 253 W. 138th Street. The spirits are here, I feel connected. I feel W. C. Handy and Eubie Blake who lived on this block. It's all here. So I feel very fortunate that I know that I am connected to this community in a major way.

 TIE IT ALL IN...

1. Who was your first male role model?
2. Did you ever thank that person for impacting your life? If yes, how? If no, why not?
3. Young men are in need of approachable male role models. Do you mentor young men in your church, community, or family?
4. As a young man have you identified a role model and determined why they fit the bill?

A = AUTHORITY

"If you wish to know what a man is,
place him in authority"
-Yugoslavian proverb

God has given man dominion and authority on earth. And it is our God given responsibility to walk in that authority. Men should not be satisfied unless they create for themselves a reputation that invokes a level of authority and respect amongst their peers and in their family. Authority carries both social and psychological depth. From a social perspective, we can be born into authority to the likes of the British Royal Family. Psychologically, parents have authority over their children. Teachers have authority in their classroom. Pastors have authority within their congregations and so on. Such psychological authority needs to be validated by some title or act of leadership so that those people who are under your authority will inevitably follow you.

I believe that a person with authority has the power to evoke change in the area over which they have dominion. Using a parent as an example, you have a voice in the image your children adopt. You have an obligation to allow your children to express their own individuality and creativity, yet exercise your authority when their image does not speak to their destiny. As parents there are certain limitations you have to set for your children. For example, parents should check their children's appearance before they leave the house. If they are not dressed appropriately explain the importance of their image and how it is a reflection on the entire family. The bottom line is as long as your son is under your roof and you are the primary provider of food, clothing, and shelter, there is absolutely no reason why your son should walk around with his pants literally down below his butt—with a belt on! No one should ever want their son to be caught with his pants down!

TIE IT ALL IN...

1. Do the people under your authority respect you?
2. Do the people under you follow you out of fear or admiration?
3. When you speak, do others listen?

G = GENEROSITY

"You make a living by what you get.
You make a life by what you give."
-Winston Churchill, Orator, Strategist, Politician

When you begin to walk in the image of God and make a conscious effort to take on His characteristics you strive to be generous as well. Many people don't know that *generous* is derived from the Latin word *generosus* which means having qualities attributed to people of noble birth; noble-minded; gracious; unselfish. Therefore as noble-minded men, we must be willing to give of both ourselves and our resources to others.

We live in a capitalistic society where money and possessions are endless. The more we get the more we want. We must resist the temptation to hoard things for ourselves and get away from the "every man for himself" philosophy. As men we must learn that money is *currency* and that it is intended to flow. The more you give to others, the more you position yourself to receive. I am not saying that you should not enjoy the fruit of your labor, but I am convinced that what you make happen for someone else, God will make happen for you. The most affluent people in this country are some of the greatest philanthropists, and that's not just for tax purposes. When they begin to give they automatically set themselves up for the abundance, and their wealth becomes generational. A wise man creates an inheritance for his children and his children's children. As you become a generous man I am confident that your grandchildren will be eternally grateful for you giving nature. What man would not be proud to hear that?.

 TIE IT ALL IN...

1. Do you find yourself often thinking about the needs of others? Are you pondering how you can help their situation?
2. What percentage of money and assets do you donate to a charity, community, or church?
3. Do you volunteer your time as a mentor, coach, tutor, etc?

E = EXCELLENCE

"Excellence is to do a common thing in an uncommon way"
—Booker T. Washington, Political Leader,
Educator, Author

Excellence is the drive for a life above average. It is something men should constantly strive for. Excellence requires superior performance. In all you do, do things with a spirit of excellence. What does that mean? It means your home is always in order. I'm not saying everyone should turn into a neurotic Felix Unger type, but if you strive to do things that are routine, yet critical to helping you become the best you can be, you have a greater chance of reaching your goal. Further, for example, take time to pray each day, whatever time works for you. Make the bed each morning. Wash the dishes each night before you go to bed. When you take authority and set your house in order, you are on track to laying a foundation for the pursuit of excellence. Take time for your personal appearance. Have you ever thought about coming to work 20 minutes early each day? Excellence means taking little steps to get better at each aspect of your life. Go ahead make every effort to be the best husband, father, neighbor, boss, employee that you can be. If you know your wife likes flowers, why not sign up with the florist and have them sent to her bi-monthly? With regard to your work ethic, meet deadlines, come in early, be a team player, and respect your colleagues. If we think of image in this context then we are on the right track to being positive examples for other men to emulate. Overall, excellence is an attitudinal decision. It is a level of personal accountability without supervision. Everyone has areas that they can work on to achieve excellence. It is important to recognize those weak spots and move towards improvement as soon as possible.

 TIE IT ALL IN...

1. Identify three areas in your life that you can sharpen?
2. Do you pay attention to detail?
3. Do you go the extra mile on projects, while cleaning, in relationships, etc.?

Chapter 6

TAKE ME BACK

"I swear to the Lord,
I still can't see, Why
Democracy means,
Everybody but me"
-Langston Hughes, Poet, Novelist

I HAVE BEEN FASCINATED WITH the period between the 1920s and 1930s in Harlem, New York because of the cultural movement and sense of freedom for Blacks and West Indians. Despite protests for equality, it was a period when blacks migrated North from rural South to make a better life for themselves. This time was commonly referred to as The Harlem Renaissance. Harlem's Black and West Indian population in the 1930s was approximately 200,000. When I look at the history and Black culture during The Harlem Renaissance, it inspires me to do more, to be the best I can be. This era brought about a time of uniqueness in being Black. Everything was new. The art, jazz music, fashion and literature spearheaded a cultural shift. The Cotton Club, one of the most prominent cabarets of our time, which launched the careers of Duke Ellington and Cab Calloway still flourishes today. This era saw more short stories, novels, plays and poems by blacks than ever before. There was a black elite list that included the likes of Langston Hughes, Claude McKay, Zora Neale Hurston, Countee

Cullen, A'Lelia Walker, and Adam Clayton Powell Jr.

Men from *The Harlem Renaissance* had an internal pride that just doesn't exist in many of the lives of men both young and old today. Despite societal pressure, ridicule, and blatant racism there was an internal pride that allowed men to weather any storm. It provoked them to leave the house with a suit and tie on. Although he might be hosed down on the way to work, he walked with his head up. It pushed him to wear a hat and jacket even if he couldn't sit at the counter at the local diner or take a front seat on the bus downtown. Today we have the freedom to come and go as we please and we leave our homes with no consciousness of who we represent. We must still be mindful that not only do we represent ourselves, but our families and our people.

It was a privilege to sit face-to-face with the "Father of Swing Dance," Mr. Clyde Wilder, Creator of the Harlem Swingers Dance Group in 1977. Mr. Wilder was a leading contributor to the choreography of the era and continues to teach and promote swing dance at the ripe age of 54.

A.E.: Recently two rappers did a movie called *Idlewild* which captured a moment in the Renaissance Era. Are you familiar with the movie?

<u>Clyde Wilder:</u> Yes, last year I got a call to bring some of my people down and we auditioned. They picked a woman from my group, Janice Loraine, she's one of the main characters in the movie.

<u>A.E.:</u> When I watch *Idlewild*, or when I think about the era in which you've danced, they weren't just average dancers. Not only were you well gifted in the art and craft of dancing but was most intriguing was the image of the dancers and the people from that era. You know, men wore spats, shined shoes, braces and hats. The ladies had on dresses, high heeled shoes, and impeccable style. Can you speak about the image from that day?

Clyde Wilder: Most of the dance fashion and the image of the people of that time were people who were highly proud of themselves and wanted to be shown in their best light all the time so they would dress their best on Sunday for the Harlem parade. Everybody dressed up and went to 125th street especially around April because of Easter. Our fashion has always come from Harlem. Harlem sort of set the mode for the fashion for that day. At the time a lot of designers and other people came up to Harlem, to the Savoy Ballroom, Smalls Paradise and the Cotton Club. They wanted to see what the fashion was going to be and it set the tone for many, many, years. Even dignitaries came to Harlem to see what the latest fashion was going to look like.

A.E.: You mentioned something very important and that was pride. Where did that pride come from that inspired a group of African Americans to dress in such a classy, elegant way?

Clyde Wilder: Despite the little bit of money and things that we did have, the pride came from the fact that we had family. You wanted to show good for your family. You wanted to be the best for your people and that was very important. Anytime an image of black people came on television we wanted to make sure that was the best image you could find. So, the word would get around when we were on television and we would say "Is that a black person on television?" and everybody would tune in to see you and to know what you were wearing so they could do the same thing. Back then you had to shine your shoes, clean your shirts, put your suit up and dust it off the night before. There was a certain order to follow when you had your father and grandfather with you. You've seen the images of guys cleaning and grooming themselves. I'm not even sure where it has gone, but we really need to work on getting it back because that's so important.

A.E.: How do you think that we can recapture that again?

Clyde Wilder: You know there were good images in the film *Idlewild.* There was a scene, even though it was harsh, where the father was talking to his son about the ethics in his work. That scene was extremely important, and the images of the film is also important. When Cicely Tyson was coming down the road and she had just went on blind faith because she knew God was going to take care of her. You know that's an image that it is planted, that's a seed in somebody's mind. That's a seed that I've been living by. And even just to do this interview here I know that it's cool to do that. You know what I mean? So I'm saying that the image of having an understanding on media in film sometimes sparks something in people and changes their thinking. It gives them another level of understanding of things.

Being a renaissance man is not a destination, it's a lifestyle. It's a way of life. It's the way you think. It's not a period. A renaissance man is always in process, always evolving. He never arrives and parks. He always maintains the posture of a student, willing to learn about different cultures, ideas, and traditions. The world is always evolving and changing and if the world is changing, you have to as well. But maintaining the right image should be constant.

Fashion designer, television personality and author Lloyd Boston is also a fan of *The Harlem Renaissance Era* and he described its influence on his style and life.

A.E.: Who influenced your image?

Lloyd Boston: I always loved the way men of color dressed in the 1900's. From the same point of view for each decade, we helped carve out fashion as it relates to American style. I love to think about the 1930's and *The Harlem Renaissance,* men like Langston Hughes strolling down Lenox Avenue looking their best. There was a certain attention to detail that wasn't about status, designer labels, or imported clothing. It was about a certain pride and an awareness of feeling and looking your best when society did not give you a reason to do so. I think our image in those days and still today is one of the few things that we really owned and controlled. The world saw us with so many different stereotypes placed upon us. So I think that image was really important because when these guys were wearing "hand me down" clothes created at local tailor shops or tailored by their mother that gave them pride in their image. It wasn't what they were wearing, it was how they wore them: how their hat was angled, how their pants were tapered and how their cuffs were hemmed. It may not have been the best of clothes, but they had a certain sense of panache which came from their fight for survival and that struggle. I think it really set the stage for the decades that followed. There's always a sense of self-empowered entitlement that comes through clothing that black men have really owned and that has inspired me growing up. Whether I was reading 'Essence' or 'Ebony Man' in the '80s I would see black icons that understood that although we didn't have hundreds of dollars we've always held on to a certain direction of style that hasn't changed.

A.E: Do you think that we've lost that sense of dignity? I think there was a sense of class and pride that we seem to have lost.

Lloyd Boston: I don't know if we've necessarily lost it especially at a time when America is becoming more casual in general. On the sportswear side, I think we've gotten more relaxed in American culture. As a global culture people aren't as formal as they once were. There are men in their '80s now wearing beautiful ornate hats as they drive to church on Sundays and wearing three piece suits that are out of style to the masses. Then you'll see the young guys wearing casual attire clothes in places where other folks might be more dressed up because that's what they're feeling. I think as a casual society it's difficult to say that we lost it, it's probably easier to say that everyone has kind of fell back a bit. It may be a little more obvious for us cause we've always been known to be a little bit more dressed up on certain occasions because we've had to understand that when we walk into a room for an interview, or in a bank for a mortgage or for a meeting of the minds, what we choose to wear is our calling card and it speaks to the other person before we have the chance to speak. Hopefully it's a kind of leveling device, an equalizer that we can be a little more casual these days. Maybe the levels of the playing field are a little bit more balanced. It may be good that we ease up a little to understand the core values of getting dressed up and what is appropriate.

Langston Hughes (1902-1967),
Poet, Novelist, Short Story Writer best known for work during Harlem Renaissance.
His poetry and fiction depicted the struggles, joy and laughter of working class
blacks in America.

A. Phillip Randolph (1889-1979),
Prominent Civil Rights Spokesman, Organizer of Brotherhood of Sleeping Car
Porters, Founded Leadership Conference on Civil Rights; Organized March on
Washington in 1963 with
Dr. Martin Luther King Jr.

Cab Calloway (1907-1994),
Jazz singer and band leader with masterful scat-singing.

Alex Ellis, CEO of Simply Ellis.
Modern Day Renaissance Man.

Chapter 7

THE POWER OF THE MEDIA

THE MEDIA HAS AND always will have an overwhelming influence on image. Whether its magazines, television, the internet, or other advertising outlets, what we see impacts our buying decisions and affects our thought process as to the right or wrong appearance.

Our culture is obsessed with the lives of the rich and famous. The paparazzi go to great lengths to trail the lives of our cultural icons. They follow them to restaurants, stores, and even rummage through their garbage, because covering lives of celebrities pays lucrative returns. There are dozens of magazines that give you the inside scoop on popular celebrities such as what they are wearing, the designer who made it, and how you can dress and look like them. It is easy to become enthralled with the aspects of someone else's life and believe you will have the happiness celebrities appear to have. I guess it would be nice every once in a while to go to the Oscar after party or be on the A-list for a few weeks. I might add that having a closet full of designer clothes, a mansion, and a Maybach may not be half bad. But that's not real life for the majority of us. If you can afford it, then go for it, but most working class people would be quickly headed to the poor house! If you are not careful you will accept the media's concept of image as the standard and spend your life in an attempt to look and live like a celebrity.

I sat down with a male high school student from Levittown, Pennsylvania to discuss his viewpoint on the image of the younger generation.

A.E.: What is your perspective on the image of the next generation, especially with the fascination with hip hop and music videos?

Emmanuel: When I watch TV and see videos with artists driving fancy cars and throwing loose money around I feel like, man if I could throw around money like this five minute video and not go to college I would be all right. I could drive a Mercedes Benz and make $60,000 dollars right after high school. I feel that hip hop has a major influence on us as a younger generation because we want to be part of the whole thing.

A.E.: Do you believe that your image today will affect your future?

Emmanuel: I believe my image will affect my future because people judge you by first impressions. First impressions are lasting impressions and I feel that if people see me now maybe they will speculate on how I'm going to be when I get older and that may not be true.

A.E.: What do you think is the responsibility of the older generation to the younger generation with reference to image?

Emmanuel: I would say the responsibility is to warn us about how things we see on television are not all they are cracked up to be. For example the cars and jewelry don't necessarily belong to the people who have them on in the videos. They should remind us that we really need to go to school, dress up for an interview and to carry ourselves with dignity and hold our heads up high. They need to remind us that we should want more out of life and strive to be successful.

HIP HOP 360°

It's been over twenty years now and it is safe to say that hip hop is not the fad it once was during its infancy stages of *Rapper's Delight*. Hip hop has become mainstream. It is not just rap music, it is a culture. Popular artists are doing business on a corporate level requiring them to take on a business suit image as opposed to a more casual look. Hip hop artists are not only performing on stages but they are performing well in the board rooms and making multimillion dollar deals outside of their musical talents. Mainstays in the industry such as Russell Simmons are not only keeping the music alive, but the culture as well. Young men today are heavily influenced by the Hip Hop Movement. It is so much more than just music, hip hop has influenced the generation's walk, talk and style. The hip hop style of the triple X white tees and baggy denim is not just common throughout our urban communities, but it has now become a global statement. Once a rap artist or other celebrity wears something in a video or photo shoot or at an awards show, the style spreads like wildfire and becomes an instant fashion statement.

The urban fashion industry is a $30 billion industry and climbing. The heavy hitters like Phat Farm, Sean John, FUBU, and Roca Wear all have carved their niche in the market. FUBU is the only label where the original owners were not millionaires when they began. Its founders began making hats at their home in Queens, New York. Hats turned to T-shirts, rugby shirts, jerseys and baseball caps. What I like most about FUBU is that they all saw the need to create a more sophisticated line of clothing for men which includes suits. All of the hip hop heavies saw the need to branch off into other lines for women, children, shoes, cologne, and accessories.

I am a fan of the new look of hip hop and hope that the younger generation begins to adopt the stylish line of suits by the prominent hip hop designers that have become staples in the closets of professional men around the world. We need to encourage young men to wear suits on dates, to church, and to other events.

THE BUSINESS OF BASKETBALL

"There are some battles in life that you just can't try to fight.
Guys make enough money to put on some dress clothes.
My plan this year was to dress up anyway. I have
40 to 50 suits already. I should be one of the
best-dressed guys this year"
- Jermaine O'Neal, NBA Player

Athletes and preferential treatment go hand in hand. Whatever the working class population is required to do, athletes just don't have the same stipulations; until now. Thanks to NBA Commissioner David Stern, the NBA has a dress code. I believe the code was long overdue. It seemed that there was a disconnect between work and play. For the average guy, shooting hoops is definitely an extracurricular activity. For a NBA player, shooting hoops is a career that pays millions of dollars a year. So why not dress for work? After all, the NBA is a corporation.

"Section 1 of the General Policy states that players are required to wear 'Business Casual' attire whenever they are engaged in team or league business." The key word here is "business." Every time a player steps on the court he is performing work for his employer, which will ultimately affect the revenue of the corporation. The Commissioner's ruling has been met with a great deal of opposition—namely players. "I think it's wrong. You shouldn't judge a person from what they wear" stated Allen Iverson. Tim Duncan, also a critic of the policy said, "I think it's a load of crap. I understand what they're trying to do with forbidding hats and do rags. That's fine. But I don't understand why they would take it to this level." Excerpts from the player dress code are as follows:

Section 1, General Policy defines 'Business Casual' as (i) A long or short-sleeved dress shirt (collared or turtleneck), and/or a sweater; (ii) Dress slacks, khaki pants, or dress jeans; (iii) Appropriate shoes and socks, including dress shoes, dress boots, or other presentable shoes, but not including sneakers, sandals, flip-flops, or work boots. There are reasonable exceptions to the code such as for special events or appearances by players. Some of the excluded items are chains, pendants, or medallions worn over the player's clothes, sunglasses while indoors, and headphones (except on team plane, bus, or locker room).

Overall, I believe the dress code is a necessity. With the majority of the NBA players representing the black community, it is good that the world see these young men in a more positive professional image. Professional athletes do not realize that they are some of the most influential role models, whether they want to be or not, in the eyes of young males. They have a responsibility to present an image that speaks to the future and destiny of the next generation.

THE RIGHT TIME, THE RIGHT PLACE

(i) Interviews / Workplace

For those of you who are serious about success, you know that you've got to dress the part. That doesn't mean you have to spend a fortune on your wardrobe, but it does mean that you are aware that your appearance affects the impression that people get from you. Interviewers say that long before an interviewer starts a dialogue concerning the candidates employment history they have made an assessment already solely based on the candidate's appearance. According to Image Dynamics out of Dallas Texas, 55% of another person's perception of you is based on how you look.

Today many corporations have embraced a business casual dress code which emerged in the early '90s in the IT world. The leaders in Silicon Valley allowed for a slightly more relaxed work attire based on the type of jobs held as most people were sitting in front of a computer several hours a day. However, even with this modification in attire there is still a standard that must be met such as no jeans or sleeveless shirts. As a rule of thumb, if you are unaware of what the dress code is for a particular corporation, it is always best to err on the side of being conservative. For men this means a dark suit, a white shirt and dress shoes.

(ii) *School*

President Clinton endorsed school uniforms for the purpose of student safety in the 1996 State of the Union Address, stating, "And if it means that teenagers will stop killing each other over designer jackets, then our public schools should be able to require their students to wear school uniforms." Following the endorsement from President Clinton and other publicity advocating school uniforms, instances of stricter dress codes (unofficial uniforms) and required uniforms increased. Urban districts with higher occurrences of gang violence and other districts wanting students to "dress for success" adopted standardized dress codes or uniform requirements; the largest percentages of 2000 included New York City, Philadelphia, Miami, Chicago, San Francisco, Boston, Cincinnati, Cleveland, and New Orleans. In urban and rural schools alike, implementation of uniforms continues to increase.

Numerous reasons can be supplied to argue for school uniforms as an aid to achieve its educational purpose: (a) to increase school attendance, (b) lessen distractions, (c) to increase student self esteem, (d) to decrease clothing costs, (e) to improve classroom behavior, and (f) to remove some causes of crime, violence, and gang activity.

For those young people who do not wear school uniforms, it is critical that parents instill valuable tips such as wearing clothes that are neatly pressed and fit comfortably. It is important to always look presentable even if you are just going to class. However, the main goal in going to school is to learn - it is not to be the best dressed. If you go with a focus to impress people with what you have on you lose sight of the bigger picture and that is your education.

(iii) <u>*The Church*</u>

Many churches today have also relaxed their dress code. Some have gone as far as instituting a casual attire at all times. The pastor might even preach in a polo shirt and khakis or even a sweat suit. Other churches have embraced a dress down Sunday where once a month they allow the membership to wear casual attire. The more traditional churches have stayed away from this fad and continued the formal attire for their services.

Casual church attire will have a huge impact on the next generation. Young people need to know that there is a level of respect they must have for the house of God, and the importance of looking presentable. This is even more crucial today in light of the fact that there are so many single parents, absentee fathers, and young kids having babies. Therefore, we have a lack of home training, and the other place for this type of training is found in the church. Like many people, I received my training for dressing appropriately in church. It taught young men how to tie a tie and enforced the need for a black suit. As a young man, a black suit is essential. It is the uniform worn whether he ushers or sings in the choir. Nowadays young men go to church without ever owning a suit. Instead, they come in wearing the latest jeans, t-shirts, and hoodies. It is important that parents, pastors and other ministerial leaders emphasize to the younger generation that even if they are dressing down, they still must look presentable—not like they are going to the park to play. This is not to negate the fact that God does not look at our outward appearance and looks at the heart. The point I want to make is that when you enter into the house of God, you should enter with a suitable appearance to show respect.

This is a subject with which Arch Bishop Delano Ellis is very familiar:

A.E.: Bishop, what do you think about the dress code in our society where everything has become business casual. It has even infiltrated into the church where most houses of worship have just taken a business casual or "come as you are" type of dress code for the church. How do you feel about this shift?

Arch Bishop Delano Ellis: Well, I think the church is hypocritical because you dress up for other things and come to church and look like you just rolled out of bed before the King of Kings. When you go to the White House you dress up. When you go to court you try to impress the jury by wearing a suit and tie. Parents let the kids come to church looking like a ragamuffin, going before God Almighty. And I think, in the summertime people relax a bit more. I just think that when people come to church they should be clean, do their hair and put on their niceties.

In addition to Arch Bishop Ellis' perspective on dressing for church, I asked Voza Rivers about how the church played a part in shaping his image as a young man.

Voza Rivers: The church was very important. I am not a regular practitioner of Sunday services but I am definitely a practitioner of the benefits of spirituality and respect that our ministers in our churches have played. There is a dynamic that has taken place with super churches. From my early humble beginnings in the Catholic church and then converting to Baptist, I have an indelible impression about how important those early gatherings and involvement with the church was in my life. The kind of respect I learned in those Sunday school classes still play a role in my life today. When I interact with people who are regular church goers I feel very positive about the roles the church plays. My son for example has just moved to Tennessee to start a church, and he is now studying to be an ordained minister after being chef for many years. I watch my son and see how he has grown to be the person that he is I know that God has watched over him and has given him a message that He's going to follow up on.

Although many people view the traditional church as a Broadway show with elaborate hats and clothing, I beg to differ. Dressing up for church taught young ladies how to carry themselves as young ladies, and the same for young men. When a young lady wears a dress she walks different, and she sits different, there is a different kind of confidence or demeanor because of her attire. When a young man wears a suit and dress shoes, he can't just play around like he would if he had on jeans and sneakers. So he has a different conduct and presence based on more classy attire. This is what we are missing in our aim to "reach" the young people. We are minimizing or totally overlooking the fact that there are some major fundamental benefits to us dressing up sometimes when we come to church. I am not advocating banning dress down Sunday's or relaxed attire, just don't miss the opportunity to teach a younger and sometimes older generation a lesson on image that they just might not get anywhere else.

PART III

ASK ALEX...

Chapter 8

FADS VS. TIMELESS FASHION

*"Fashion is a form of ugliness so intolerable that
we have to alter it every six months."*
-Oscar Wilde, Playright

WEBSTER'S DICTIONARY DEFINES A fad as a custom, style that many people are interested in for a short time; a passing fashion craze. When you are looking to establish the well-rounded wardrobe you must make sound shopping decisions. Unless you hit the lottery, the average person does not have the money to go out and buy a new wardrobe in one shot. You can build a wardrobe one piece at a time. And that's not necessarily a bad thing; you just have to make wise choices.

In fashion there are always fads, which is a particular style that is followed for a time with exaggerated zeal. In the '70s, we had psychedelic colors and bell bottomed pants. In the '80s, we had florescent colors and mini skirts. The '90s brought a grunge look. Although we are all tempted to run out and buy these cool pieces it ends up being a mistake because these trendy pieces are short lived. So even if you get it on sale at the end of the season, by the time next year rolls around those items are out of style and you have just invested money in something that is no longer in style. I would encourage you to purchase pieces that are classic and timeless in style so that five years from now you know it will still be stylish.

Classic pieces are timeless articles of clothing that are essential to every individual's wardrobe. For example a navy blue blazer for a man will never go out of style and can be worn in a variety of ways. As opposed to a zoot suit that might be in this year, but chances are next year another color or fabric could very well be in and your outfit is now out of style. Classic pieces are those that have stood the test of time. Don't get me wrong. It's okay to get a trendy piece here or there, but never over saturate your wardrobe with those items, because when they go out of style your entire wardrobe is now out of style.

Style is one part of your shopping consideration, but you must also consider the quality. People often purchase clothing solely based on price, and sometimes that lower priced garment is inferior in quality. Subsequently the longevity of the garment is very short. You will do better in the long run to buy fewer quality pieces, as opposed to a lot of cheap things. By the time you keep replacing cheap clothing that wears out and comes apart easily, you could have spent the extra money investing in a more expensive, quality garment.

People often ask me if they have to have a lot of money to have a nice wardrobe, and my response is not necessarily. Of course it is much easier with more money, but it is not a necessity. For those on a budget, I would suggest that you start going to quality, high-end stores. I know many people are so intimidated that they won't even go into certain stores. They feel that they are out of their league. But you will never know what the next level looks like if you never see it. Even the most exclusive stores have sales at the end of the season. If you hold out to the end of the season you can pick up some quality garments at a fraction of the cost, and since you are buying classic pieces, they are sure to be in style next year. If you get a major piece each season, before you know it you will have a quality well rounded wardrobe.

Chapter 9

THE GENTLEMEN'S
WARDROBE BASICS

MEN OFTEN ASK ME how they can establish a new wardrobe. They may have received a promotion on their job or they just might want to take their image to the next level. I often tell them that a quality wardrobe takes time to build. Now of course if an elderly relative left you an inheritance, then by all means you can go right out and purchase an entirely new wardrobe. But if the inheritance is not in your future, you must focus on the right purchases to build your new look. I have devised what I call "The Gentlemen's Wardrobe Basics" to help you get started.

Let me begin by saying, men at times see other stylish men or even a store mannequin, and they are eager to run to duplicate a jazzy outfit. Generally that might not necessarily be a bad selection, if you have already covered your basics. The problem I find is that men sometimes start with an eccentric suit that stands out every time they wear it, and if that is your only suit you really limit how often you can wear it again without people saying, "Hey that's a nice distinct suit I saw you in the other day." I would recommend that you go with something solid so that you can change your shirt and tie and literally look like you have a totally different ensemble every time you wear it. Then as your wardrobe grows feel free to add more non-traditional suits.

Essential to every man's wardrobe is a navy blue or black suit. This is appropriate for any interview, religious service, or funeral. Remember these are your foundational pieces so stay away from colored stripes initially. There should also be no more than four buttons on a single breasted suit. Another important point to note is that when a man stands straight with his hands at his side, clinches his fist, the bottom of his suit jacket should fall into the fold of his hands. This will help you determine if your jacket length is too long or too short.

Along with this suit a gentleman needs a couple of quality dress shirts. I would suggest white and light blue for starters. If you have never tried a French cuff shirt, now is the time to give it a try. It is guaranteed to take your look to another level of class. French cuff shirts are amazing because your cuff links are an added detail that gives your outfit a special flair. A pair of silver or gold cuff links is a good selection for your first pair since they can compliment any shirt and tie combination. Make sure your shirts are 100% cotton and not a blend, so they will have greater durability, and less wrinkles.

Blazers are also essential to a gentleman's wardrobe. There are times when a suit is not required, but yet you need more than just a shirt and slacks, and the blazer is the answer. I would recommend a solid navy blue or camel colored jacket. These two colors are classics and can be readily found in most men's boutiques or department stores. You will undoubtedly be able to match these blazers up with a number of trousers.

A pair of solid navy, heather grey or tan slacks would be excellent to interchange with your blazers and give you a large variety of looks with a tie, bowtie, or even a turtleneck. You also need a good pair of khaki's, preferably ones that don't have pockets on the side of the legs like cargo pants, remember these are your foundational pieces.

A pocket square is also a great accent to a man's blazer, and since we are building a foundation I would recommend a white cotton pocket square, which can go with any outfit. Pocket squares are also a sign of a man of distinction. The details truly make the difference. Your pocket square does not have to be identical to your tie, but it adds flair to your ensemble. There are several ways to wear the pocket square. You can fold it into a square, tuck in the pointed edges and show a puff, or tuck in the puff and let the pointed ends stick out. A gentleman's pocket square should never hang too far out of his pocket. Remember the pocket square is an accessory not the main event. Please stay away from ready made pocket squares that have a cardboard bottom! Distinguished gentlemen wear full pocket squares even if they have to invest in a book that shows them how to properly wear it.

In today's world you also need a few polo shirts for your casual events or if you have to run to the mall or take care of some errands on the weekend. A gentleman also needs a sharp pair of jeans. They should not be too fitted or too oversized. They should comfortably rest on your shoe or sneaker, but there should not be so much fabric by your ankles that they drag the floor. The jeans should also be plain without a lot of writing on them or colorful stitch. The current trend allows you to interchange with your blazers as well for a more casual chic look.

Finally, let's discuss your footwear. The unanimous choice is black shoes. A pair of black leather shoes is a must have. Try to stay away from extremes—namely extremely square or pointed fronts. Make sure you treat your leather shoes with shoe cream, the better you are to them, the better they will be to you. If you take short cuts and just use black liquid polish, you will get done quicker but they have a tendency to crack or peel over time. Also get taps on the front and back of your shoes. This helps them look better longer, and it saves you money. Instead of having to replace a heel on a shoe because it has been worn down, you only have to replace a tap. Also, pick up a nice pair of loafers or casual dress shoes for those times when you wear business casual attire. This will save on the wear and tear of your black dress shoes and compliment the casual ensemble.

I hope this has been helpful in laying a solid wardrobe

foundation. These are not the only options, but they are definitely a start for any man who is serious about establishing a gentleman's wardrobe.

Chapter 10

Dressing For
the Occasion

CHURCH SERVICE - TIP: KNOW THE HOUSE RULES

HERE IS NO BLANKET response to the well-dressed man dressing for a religious service. There are many houses of worship that require a more traditional form of dress for their services. In that case a suit, shirt, tie, pocket square, and leather soled dress shoes would be most appropriate. Rubber sole shoes should be reserved for casual events.

If a house of worship has adopted an informal dress code, then a well-dressed man would do well to wear a blazer, shirt (long sleeve or polo), slacks, and a pocket square. Always remember that the details make the difference. The addition of adding a pocket square is a detail that distinguishes a well-dressed man.

FUNERAL – TIP: FADE TO BLACK

It is important to remember when dressing for a funeral service that you always want to give your deepest respect to the occasion which you are participating in. Therefore, your attire should be one that does not draw attention to yourself. Your most somber attire is recommended. Whether you are just attending the service or are part of the bereaved family the appropriate attire for well-dressed man is a dark suit, black or navy suit, a white freshly laundered shirt, a tie (preferably one that has a subtle color if any), a pocket square and a pair of well-shined black shoes.

DATE / NIGHT ON THE TOWN – TIP: YOU CAN NEVER GO WRONG WITH A BLAZER

When preparing to go out on a date most women spend hours preparing themselves. I by no means want to encourage a man to do the same, however, there is a principle that women impart that is important for men to take note of. Women do all they can to look their best for the person that they are going to be with. Men on the other hand could stand to take a little more time in their preparation. Remember first impressions are lasting impressions whether you are on an interview or date. Besides it makes the person that you are with feel special knowing that you cared enough about them to look sharp.

Depending on where the date is, certain restaurants require a jacket, in which case a well-dressed man should at least wear a blazer, collared shirt, slacks and shoes. If you are going to some place a little less formal, slacks, a shirt, and a pair of casual shoes should suffice. If by chance you decide to wear jeans they should be a pair of dressy jeans. Jeans have now become more mainstream, however, it is important to note if you are going out, the pair of jeans you choose to wear should not be the same jeans you wear around the house, to class, or to do yard work. You should have a pair of really nice jeans that you reserve for the times you are going out.

JOB INTERVIEW – TIP: ERR ON THE SIDE OF CONSERVATISM

Dressing for an interview should be taken very seriously. No matter what the position is an interviewer automatically gives credibility to a well-dressed man. Let me first encourage you to do your homework. Find out what the dress code is for that company. Clearly the dress code at a high school is different than that of a law firm, but you always want to put your best foot forward. If it calls for traditional business attire, you should wear a business suit (preferably navy or grey), a pressed white or light blue shirt, a pair of black polished shoes, a white pocket square, and a tie (subtle colors are always safe).

BARBEQUE – TIP: A POLO SHIRT & KHAKI SHORTS ALWAYS WORK

One sign of a well-dressed man is having a balanced wardrobe. Just as you do not want to be under dressed for a formal affair, you also do not want to be over dressed for an informal occasion. With that in mind, a well-dressed man should wear a polo shirt or even a t-shirt (preferably one that is not overly saturated with logos or words). He should also wear a pair of khaki's or shorts that are clean and neatly pressed, even if they do not have a crease. Finally there are some great linen two piece sets that are a great choice. They come either with a linen shirt and shorts or a linen shirt and pants. Either way it will keep you both cool and sharp at the same time.

WEDDING – TIP: PAY ATTENTION TO THE TIME OF DAY AND LOCATION

Wedding attire can vary depending on what time of day it is held and what type of reception the bride and groom are having. All of these details are in the invitation, so be sure to pay close attention to it. If the wedding is in the morning or early afternoon, a well-dressed man will wear a dark suit, shirt and tie. If it is in the South, at a resort, or destination wedding he can wear a dark colored linen, cotton, or seersucker suit.

If the gentleman is invited to an evening wedding after six the dark suit is still appropriate unless the invitation stipulates "black tie." In that case he should wear a black tuxedo or a black dinner jacket and black trousers. He should also have on a white formal shirt with a pair of cuff links, a black bowtie, tie, or ascot, a white pocket square, and highly polished pair of black shoes (or patent leather). If a gentlemen is ever in doubt concerning the appropriate attire for a wedding he should feel free to contact the host or hostess.

References

American Academy of Facial Plastic & Reconstructive Surgery 2005 Membership Survey: Trends in Facial Plastic Surgery, Magnet Communications, February 2006.

Bixler, Susan and Rice Nix, Nancy, *The New Professional Image, 2nd Edition.* Masssachusetts: Adams Media, 2005.

Eldredge, John, *Wild At Heart, Discovering The Secret of A Man's Soul.* Nashville: Thomas Nelson, Inc., 2001.

Greene, Robert, *The 48 Laws of Power.* New York: Penguin Books, 2000.

Jackson, Caroline, "The Harlem Renaissance, Pivital Period in the Development of Afrian American Culture," in Yale New-Haven Teachers Institute Curriculum Unit 78.02.03 [Available online]

Kramer, Peter, *Against Depression.* New York: Penguin Books, 2005.

Munroe, Myles, *Understanding the Purpose and Power of Men.* New Kensington: Whitaker House, 2001.

NBA.com.Regulations.Player Dress Code. [Available online]

Zdenek, Marilee, Founder and President of Right Brain Resources, Inc., Santa Barbara, CA.

http://sports.espn.go.com/nba/news/story?1d=2197001 [Available online]

http://www.naesp.org/contentload.do?contentID=929 (National Association of Elementary and Public Schools. [Available online])

About the Author

ALEX ELLIS

ALEX ELLIS, A NATIVE of Hillside, New Jersey desires to do all things in Christ with the spirit of excellence. Ellis is currently a candidate for his Masters Degree of Theological Studies in Urban Ministries at New Brunswick Theological Seminary/ Rutgers University.

He serves as a mentor for the "Boys To Men" Program, and is the Chaplain for the Police and Fire Department in the City of New Brunswick. Ellis serves as the Assistant to Bishop George C. Searight of Abundant Life Family Worship Center in New Brunswick, New Jersey and also the Special Events Coordinator.

Ellis is CEO of Simply Ellis LLC, a custom clothing company specializing in suits, shirts, Italian neckwear, and exquisite cuff links. He is a member of the Custom Tailors and Designers Association of America. For more information about this man destined to become one of the era's leading men log on to www.simplyellis.com.

CPSIA information can be obtained
at www.ICGtesting.com
Printed in the USA
FFHW012049040519
52214159-57597FF